to Harriet, Ted and Eleanor

Text copyright © Joyce Dunbar, 1991
Illustrations copyright © James Dunbar, 1991

Photoset by Deltatype Ltd, Ellesmere Port
Printed in Italy
for J. M. Dent & Sons Ltd
91 Clapham High Street
London SW4 7TA

British Library Cataloguing in Publication Data
Dunbar, Joyce
  Why is the sky up?
  I. Title II. Dunbar, James
  823.914 [J]

The illustrations for this book were prepared using water-colour.

Why is the sky up?

Joyce & James Dunbar

Dent Children's Books · London

"Dad. Why is the day light?"

"So that we know when to get up. So that we can see. If the day was dark we'd get our clothes in a muddle."

"Dad. Why are we the right way up?"

"If we were upside down, it would be very difficult to eat breakfast. The food would all fall to the floor."

"Dad. Why is the park outside?"

"Because the park is too big to be inside. Trees don't grow in sitting-rooms. You can't have a lake indoors."

"Dad. Why is the sky up?"

"Because if the sky was down we would walk on it and trample it all over. It's so soft we might fall through."

"Dad. Why does the sun shine?"

"The sun shines to make us warm. It shines to show our shadows. Then we know what shape we are. Just think if the shapes got mixed up."

"Dad. Why do the clouds move?"

"The wind blows them along. If we were
as light as the clouds the wind
would blow us along too."

"Dad. Why does the rain fall in drops?"

"Because if the rain fell all at once we'd get very wet. We might have to swim all the way home."

"Dad. Why can't I see the stars in the day?"

"Perhaps if you could see them you'd try
to catch them and take them home.
Then the moon would be all on its own."

"Dad. Why is the moon so far away?"

"The moon is far away to make us wonder why. If the moon was near we might turn it into a car-park. Then it wouldn't be shiny any more."

"Dad. Why is the night dark?"

"So that the world knows when to go to bed, and that means you know too."

"Dad. Why is there a world?"

"Because if there wasn't a world there would be no day, no sky, no sun . . ."

"no shadows, no stars, no moon . . .
no you, no me, no questions.
Goodnight now."